tenth avenue north

THE [LIGHT MEETS] THE DARK

ISBN 978-1-4234-9419-5

HAL•LEONARD®
CORPORATION

7777 W. BLUEMOUND RD. P.O. BOX 13819 MILWAUKEE, WI 53213

Visit Hal Leonard Online at
www.halleonard.com

HEALING BEGINS

Words and Music by JASON INGRAM,
MIKE DONEHEY and JEFF OWEN

STRONG ENOUGH TO SAVE

Words and Music by MIKE DONEHEY,
JASON INGRAM and PHILLIP LaRUE

With a driving beat

You fought, __ but you were just __ too weak, __ so you lost __ __ all the things you tried __ to keep. __

YOU ARE MORE

Words and Music by JASON INGRAM
and MIKE DONEHEY

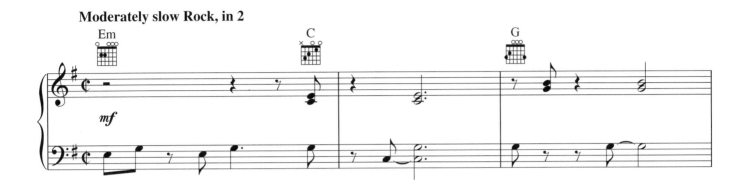

There's a girl in ____ the cor - ner

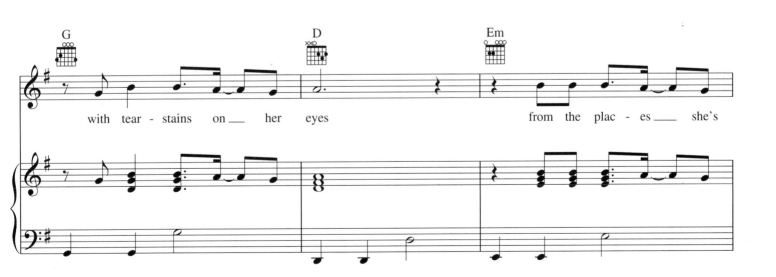

with tear - stains on ____ her eyes   from the plac - es ____ she's

THE TRUTH IS WHO YOU ARE

Words and Music by JASON INGRAM
and MIKE DONEHEY

ALL THE PRETTY THINGS

Words and Music by JASON INGRAM,
MIKE DONEHEY and JEFF OWEN

ANY OTHER WAY

Words and Music by JASON INGRAM
and MIKE DONEHEY

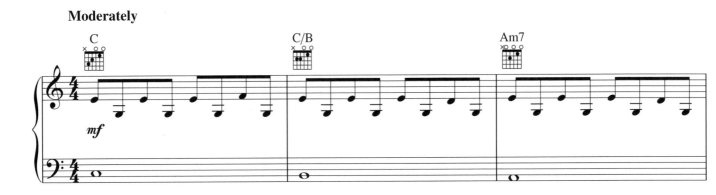

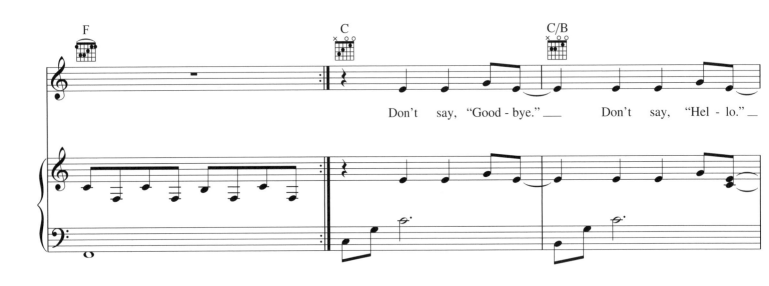

Don't say, "Good - bye." ___ Don't say, "Hel - lo." ___

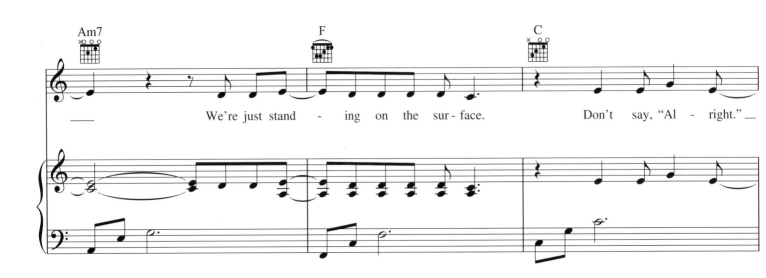

___ We're just stand - ing on the sur - face. Don't say, "Al - right." ___

ON AND ON

Words and Music by JASON INGRAM,
MIKE DONEHEY and JEFF OWEN

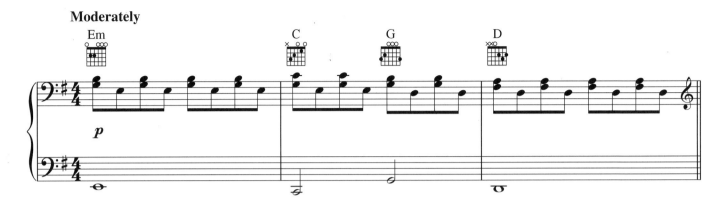

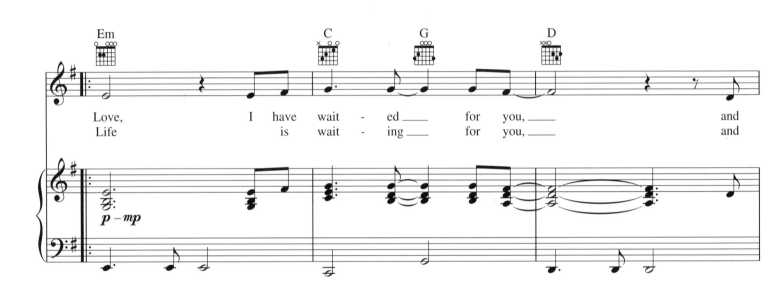

Love,   I have wait-ed ___ for you, ___   and
Life   is wait-ing ___ for you, ___   and

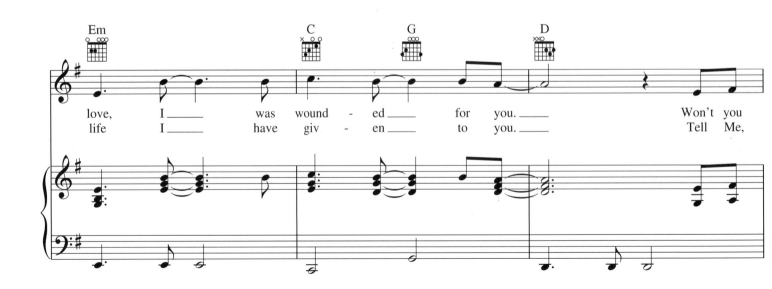

love, I ___ was wound-ed ___ for you. ___   Won't you
life I ___ have giv-en ___ to you. ___   Tell Me,

HEARTS SAFE
(A Better Way)

Words and Music by MIKE DONEHEY
and JEFF OWEN

HOUSE OF MIRRORS

Words and Music by MIKE DONEHEY,
JEFF OWEN, JASON JAMISON
and SCOTT SANDERS

* Recorded a half step lower.

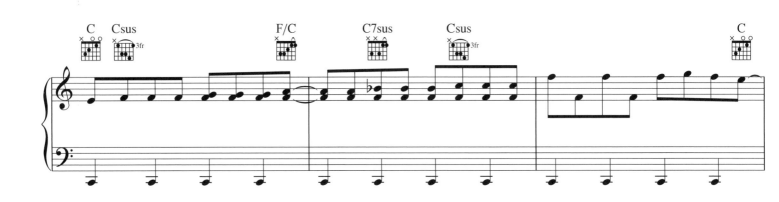

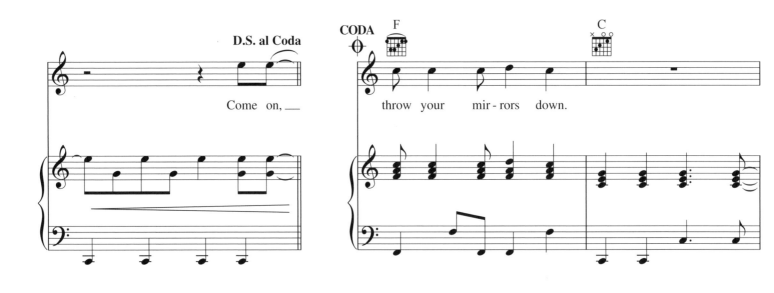

Come on, ___ throw your mir - rors down.

You've got - ta throw ___ your mir - rors down. _____ Oh, now, __

EMPTY MY HANDS

Words and Music by
MIKE DONEHEY

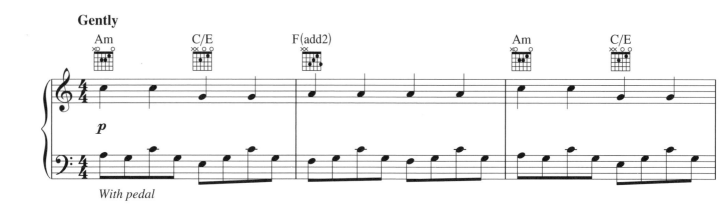

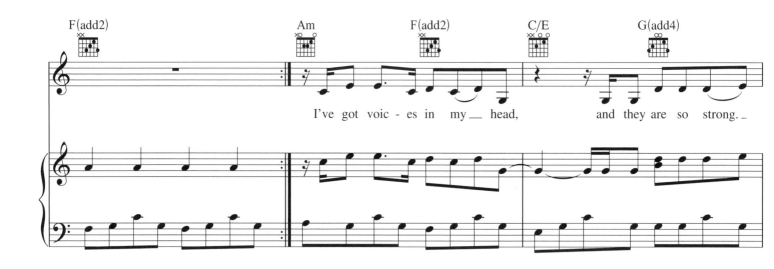

I've got voic-es in my __ head, and they are so strong. __

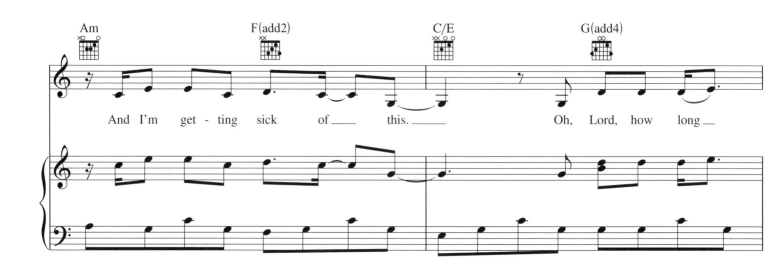

And I'm get-ting sick of ___ this. ___ Oh, Lord, how long ___

OH MY DEAR

Words and Music by MIKE DONEHEY
and GARRETT GREEN

called you up, you __ were in bed. __ Could bare - ly make out the words __ that you said. __

__ But you want - ed to see __ me in - stead, __ so I got dressed. __